*To Dalton and Momtom and everyone else
who should be too old to believe in birthdays.*

Titles in this series:
Grandmas and Grandpas
To Dad
To Mum (UK), To Mom (US)

12 11 10 9 8 7 6 5 4 3 2
Second edition published simultaneously in 1997 by Exley Publications
in Great Britain and Exley Giftbooks in the USA.
First edition published Great Britain in 1984 by Exley Publications.
First published in the USA in 1992 by Exley Giftbooks.

Copyright © Helen Exley 1984, 1997.
The moral right of the author has been asserted.
**Exley Publications Ltd, 16 Chalk Hill, Watford, Herts WD1 4BN,
United Kingdom.**
**Exley Giftbooks, 232 Madison Avenue, Suite 1206,
NY 10016, USA.**

ISBN 1-85015-842-8

Title page illustration by Samantha
Front cover illustration by Leeanne Jenkins
Back cover illustration by Elem Jones
Typeset by Delta, Watford, Herts.
Printed and bound in the UAE.

Happy Birthday!
(you poor old wreck)

EXLEY
NEW YORK • WATFORD, UK

Edited by
Helen Exley

What is a birthday?

You have a birthday every year and you can be any age and you start with being one second old.

Emma Labrum Age 7

Emma Labram Age 7

Just think, if only you could snap your fingers on the birthday you wanted and never grow any older. HUH! Birthdays won't even let you do that because you've got so much artheritis your fingers won't snap!

Susan Curzon Age 12

Growing old means that you can be young and then old but you can't grow old and then young.

Colin West Age 8

Cats have birthdays like us. No one nose what cats thik about birthdays probly nothink

Denis Hutchinson Age 8

Alexander Davenport Age 5

Take my advice and ignore birthdays unless you want to end up old and wrinkled.

Susan Curzon *Age 12*

Birthdays!

When your mother arrives home from shopping you are there waiting for her, for the first time all year, offering to unpack her bags, which she politely declines. You later sneak up to her room and peep at the interesting package under her bed and find a rain-soaked train set. You get to school late next morning because you've overslept. Your teacher promptly informs you that you are going to have to stay after school. You think "typical".

The rest of the day drags on forever until finally the last bell rings. You rush out of class, run down the stairs, trip over the bottom step, fall down and get a nose bleed. You race home in the pouring rain to a mother who is still smiling even though her new hairstyle has been ruined by the pouring rain. She lets you have a coke and far more chocolate chips than is good for you. Then you eat a large dinner and more cake than you can possibly eat (but you eat it anyway). You spend the rest of the evening trying to make the train work and go to bed feeling very sick.

Graham Munday Age 13

Birthdays are nice because you can fight your brother and he gets the blame.

Mark Scull Age 11

I always feel superior over people one year younger than myself, but if someone is one year older than me I feel small and look forward to when I will be one year older, but everyone else seems to get one year older as well.

Steven McMullan *Age 11*

A birthday is happiness all the world over.

Zoltan Jovari *Age 9*

Claire Billinghurst *Age 8*

From cradle to grave

0

I wish I could be one week old once again. You only had to cry if you wanted something done, just like shouting zap, everything is done. No worrying about homework, you just sit gurgling merrily at home.

Elizabeth Wyatt Age 9

2

My best age is 2. Everybody is kind and almost never gets mad. When you go out you are pushed

along or carried. You never have to clean your bedroom or make your bed. And you can crawl into places you aren't supposed to go.

Sarah Hill *Age 9*

8

The best age I have ever been is eight. I liked it because nobody ever said "You are two old for this" or "You are too young for that". Another reason why I liked being eight was that I felt very grown up. I do not feel grown up any more although I still feel quite a bit older than people who are eight.

Sophie McMullen *Age 9*

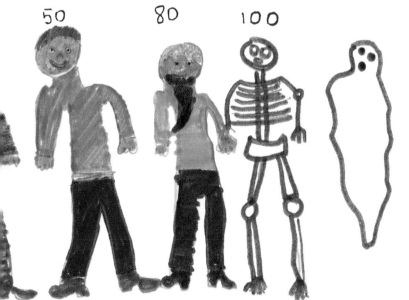

James Barker *Age 9*

17

I think the ideal age is seventeen, because you will have finished school. You could stay up late and watch horror films.

Clara McAlinden *Age 10*

19

I think 19 will be my nicest age. Then I will be rich enough to own a Jaguar, a Rolls Royce and a Mercedes.

Merry Lomax *Age 9*

When you get to 22 your hand begins to shake and you can't cut out sticky paper anymore

21

Birthdays are happy times until... you reach the biggest birthday, "The perfect age", Twentyone! Then every birthday is harder to hide. A slight crease under the eyes and then you're not twenty-one. You're old.

Sara Burnham *Age 13*

23

I would like to be about twenty-three because you are too young to have a family and too old to be fussed over by relatives.

Lowri Vernon Roberts *Age 10*

24

It would be good to stay at twenty-four. At twenty-four all the boys would be proposing marriage to me and carrying my shopping bags and take off their hats to me. They would try to win me with flattery and compliments, like saying I was the most beautiful girl in the world, I was like a gem and a sweet smelling fragrant flower.

Maria Richards *Age 11*

I think I will stay with 24, a much nicer age. I might even be married (every age has snags to it).

Jane Moriarty *Age 11*

Mark Rose *Age 7*

WHEN I am 24
I will BE old I
Will Go To
THE NURSE She gives
ME a Walking Stick.

Joanne McKinley Age 6

25

When you are about 25 you can do everything.
But you also got to do the shopping and do the
dirty work like washing dishes and the smelly
shorts.

David Loney Age 9

Middle age is wen
you Pors yor
Drivin test

Emma Newman Age 7

40

Andrew Hammond *Age 10*

Today is my fortieth birthday, and
I am beginning to look it. It's quite
an ordeal to look at my face first thing
in the morning. I wouldn't dare leave
my bedroom with my make-up off.
I might give someone a terrible scare.
Not that I look all that glamorous with my makeup
on. I suppose the trouble with me is that I am too
scared to admit that I'm middle-aged. Too scared
to face the fact that when I stop laughing the
wrinkles don't go.

Belinda Harding *Age 14*

I am forty, I am turning old. I just retired from my
job because I cannot manage going up and down
hills. I know I will soon die.

Jennifer Turner *Age 8*

50

When old people are 50 years old they start
getting crincals.

Suzanne Everitt *Age 9*

When you turn 50 years old, your bones get
creaky.

Dean Hodges *Age 9*

The only disadvantage when you are 50 or over, the brain tissue gets smaller and you start to become a litle screwy.

Mark Tychnoisky *Age 11*

55
When I am 55 I will not be able to walk.

Mark Dyson *Age 10*

When you are about 55 your bones start going very soft and just about holds you up

Darren Penn

Samantha Syer *Age 7*

60

Sixty is quite a pleasant age because you have grandchildren to spoil and buy things for. You would go on exotic journeys to Europe and the Orient. You would have to be really cheerful though because you might die the next day.

Erica Sabine *Age 10*

70

One of the saddest things of growing old is that you might have an illness that cannot be cured and the doctor might say, "We are sorry, very, very, but we are going to have to put you to sleep."

Alex Stanger *Age 7*

100

I would like to be the grand age of 100. I would like to feel I have lived a century, seen children grow up, the world changed, peace made between people who hate each other.

E. Swallow

Mark Sully *Age 10*

PS. A final thought
When you die you don't have birthdays.
David Pollick Age 7

PPS.
I would like to tell you one more thing, the middle
age always win.
Penny Sullings Age 9

Oh to be a grown-up!

I like the idea of growing old, well, not too old, about nineteen or so.

Mimi Cuthbert *Age 9*

I like growing up because when you grow up you don't have to do what your mother says.

Jason Torrington *Age 9*

I am glad that when you are old, you do not have to do homework. I am very very glad about that.

Elizabeth Fisher *Age 8*

I want to be a grown up because then I won't have to eat things that are good for me all the time.

Jaynie Hoffman *Age 10*

I never want to be a grown up. The only things I look forward to are being able to smoke legally, have sex legally, drink alcohol legally, drive, get into X-rated films legally and stay out till any time I like. Oh, and also getting more money. I could marry a millionaire, but I rather think I'll want to work instead.

Alison *Age 14*

Katie Goldtorpe *Age 7*

Old age begins at 8

When I started jogging I was three. But I can't jog so much now as I used to.

Maxine Brown *Age 8*

Everyone has a birthday each year. You are a year older, and your body gets weaker. People get weaker every year. I wouldn't like to be old. It means a lot of trouble for the young people. I soon will be an old person. I am only nine.

Lisa Beagle *Age 9*

About the birthday longest ago that I can remember is when I was seven, and that wasn't very long ago. I got about fifteen presents then and everyone loved me, now look at me. I used to have parties with lots of people there, but now I can only invite a couple of friends over and we go to McDonald's or somewhere.

Nicholas *Age 10*

When you have a birthday you feel miserable because you don't get toy cars anymore.

Michael Graham *Age 8*

Year by Year
And day by day
I'm growing older
And so I say;
I'm not as young as I'd like to be,
But in this world, who is?

Janet Smith *Age 13*

Gemma Hayward *Age 8*

Grown-ups!

Some adults do the most crazy things like going up a mountain and getting stuck in some mud, and then some more people come along and get stuck in the same lot of mud.

Marianne Wales *Age 10*

Grown up people have more chances to do things because children cannot spank grown up people.

Aike Arnheim *Age 7*

Grown-ups are always rushing around doing things like sweeping up last minute bits of dust off the floor and rushing everywhere shooing children away to school, not to mention trying to sing a baby to sleep before rushing off to a PTA meeting or running to the grocery store at closing time.

Georgina Morgan *Age 8*

If you are a grown-up you can do nearly anything you like, if it is not against the law. They can have parties, but they nearly always have a hang over. Sometimes grown-ups act stupid.

Carol Peace *Age 10*

Some grown-ups act like two-year olds

Rachel Bouness *Age 10*

Mostyn

Grown-up just means bossy

Grown-ups are like Big children, only they are bossier and they say they are always right.

Marianne Wales *Age 10*

Grown-ups always decide what we'll have to eat and they always seem to pick the thing that I do not like! I do not like the way that they treat you like worms.

Heather Dean *Age 10*

When children want to say something to adults while they are talking they tell the children not to interrupt but it seems an awful long time until they stop talking and listen to you.

Clare Theakson *Age 10*

grown up is when you can boss children around

Sara Brudenell *Age 7*   **Caroline H. Grant** *Age 8*

That dreaded 30th birthday

The first sign of growing old is needing a pair of glasses which reveals the second and third signs, the first wrinkle and the first white hair. The fourth sign is the thirtieth birthday.

Agnes Ring *Age 15*

Suddenly life is a lot harder. You become middle-aged. You get "middle-age spread". You go flabby around your waist. You do not feel quite as young and fit as you used to. Your hair either starts to go white or to fall out. Or both! But you are still growing in two ways. You are growing older and, probably, fatter.

Luisa Kate Davis *Age 12*

Martin Farrer *Age 10*

old people die
When They are
very very old
Like 50
or 4 o

Zara Bannerjee Age 5

Can you hear me?
Your going deaf,
what a shame.
Can you see me
or are you getting a bit blind?
Your face has many wrinkles
hasn't it,
now you're getting old.
That's a nice walking stick
Can't you walk without it?
You will soon be thirty
won't you?

Jane Hitchman

Mother is twenty-one again

My Mother keeps saying every year that she's twenty-one, but I'm getting a bit suspicious because she's said it for the last 12 years.

Gregory Payne *Age 11*

I love hassling my mother when it is her birthday. I keep reminding her that she is getting older and all I get is a clout on the ear!

Justin *Age 10*

Cheer up Mom, we all get old. Just look at Dad.

Dale Fagence *Age 11*

Although my mother is getting a little old she still likes to run wild on her birthday.

Gary Higson *Age 11*

If we buy her a card with 16th birthday on the front, she says, "I like you, you can have extra pocket money".

Fiona Nicholls *Age 10*

My mother said she doesn't mind *getting* older, it's *looking* older she can't stand.

Debbie Miano *Age 12*

Cheer up Mum,
don't be glum
Just think
if there was
no false teeth
All you would have
is gums.

Patricia *Age 10*

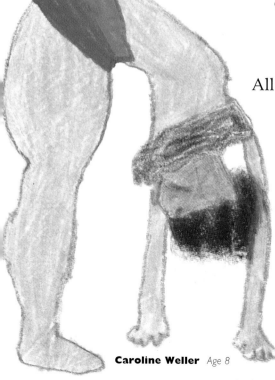

Mom trying to keep her figure young.

Caroline Weller *Age 8*

YOU'RE GOING BALD ON TOP

YOUR JACKETS BULGING AT THE SEAMS

YOU'VE GOT WRINKLES ON YOUR FACE

YOUR FINGERS ARE WORKED TO THE BONE

YOUR FEET ARE FULL OF BUNIONS.

YOU'VE DONE A HARD DAYS WORK SO...

... Don't worry dad

YOU'RE NOT AS OLD AS YOU LOOK

Matthew Bebbington Age 10

Poor old Dad!

Happy birthday dear Dad. I see you're going bald, but never mind at least you won't get head lice.

Helen Lawrence *Age 10*

It's Dad's birthday on Tuesday.
Now what shall I get him?
All his friends forgot last year
and he was very sad.
I'd like to forget my
birthday especially if I was
going to be that age.

Julie Wheeler

You know you are old when...

... you try to comb your hair so that it doesn't all fall out.

Patricia Mulqueen *Age 13*

... you hang a sock on the fireplace and Santa ignores it.

Sandra Reddy *Age 14*

... you puff and pant when you've just been around the room with the vacuum cleaner.

Patricia Mulqueen *Age 13*

You know you're *really* old when you need new false teeth because your others are too worn down!

Jane McNeill *Age 13*

Getting old is... getting white hairs from worrying about your wrinkles.

Sandra Reddy *Age 14*

You can tell when people get old. Their hair falls out and they get out of breath. They always talk about the old times and you haven't got a clue what they are talking about.

Mark Thornton *Age 11*

... you start to say things like "In my day".

Carole Waters *Age 15*

Rachel Hall *Age 8*

The symptoms...

When you are old your body creaks and your knees knock and your teeth fall out.

Adrian Tydd *Age 10*

... you get rincled skin and white hair and blood shot eyes.

Amanda Leonard *Age 11*

... you get flopy.

Timothy Ferguson

You don't rush about when you are old your knees creak We hear you coming.

Nigel Bosley *Age 10*

... you get very fat or you may get crumpled up.

Maurice Paine *Age 9*

Also when you get old you will grow bent and shrink as well and you also seem to wear scarfs and hats.

Danny Field *Age 8*

Being old is not plesent. You have wobbly knees. You have a crinckly face and a crinckly nose and your eyes begin to shut. When it comes to birthdays you get so excited your litly to have a hart attack.

Nicky H.

When you are an old man you go all crooked and you Keep falling down

Paul Hewitson *Age 8*

When you're grown up and you have a birthday you feel funny. You can't do PE any more because you can't bend over because of your fat tummy.

John Fielding *Age 8*

Old Fogies Anonymous

Remember the days you went to School, how you used to run after the girls. Now your grandson is probably doing the same. But can you do the same now? Well I've never heard of anyone running with a walking stick.

Mario Marandola Age 11

You are growing old at this second and by the time you have read this, you will be a few minutes older. Depressing, isn't it? But think of all the advantages. When you're a little old man or woman you can do whatever you like, say whatever you like and go wherever you like. If you're rude people won't mind, they'll just say you're old and your mind is wandering.

Sandra Marsden Age 13

Old ladies get mixed up with money. They give you a tiny coin and even though you won't be able to get a single ice cream you still say thank you.

Paul Hearne Age 11

Sarah Leonard Age 6

Getting older means a lot of things to me like meals-on-wheels, and bingo. But first the thing that strikes me most is wobly legs and bad backs. It also means becoming a grandfather or even a great grandfather, and if you have any children they become about thirty years old which makes you feel about four hundred.

Lee Caller Age 11

They say hello and you say hello back and they yell out WHAT!

Rachel A. Fyfe Age 10

Keep in shape old man!

When they

the hill, at least
fun going

HAPPY

Anthony Laws *Age 9*

Darren Forshaw *Age 9*

Say you're over
you can have some
down the other side
RETIREMENT

Andrew Chambers Age 13

Sarah Chadwick Age 13

MT. EVERE

The grouchers

David Oshor *Age 10*

Older people are sometimes grouchy. Most of the time when they go along the street they talk to there selfs and mumbal. They are really fussy I can tell you that. You should hear them when my mother comes in, chitt chatt chatt, they go on and on.

Helen *Age 9*

Old people complain a lot and are generally very nosey, interfering and old-fashioned. We have a lot to thank them for, so my mom says anyway.

Joanna Summers *Age 13*

Joanna Bates *Age 10*

There is an old lady who lives near me who thinks that whatever you do, you are the wrong age to do it. If you are going with your friends to a show, or a disco or something, she says you're too young. She sees you going to buy a toy though, then she says you're too old to have toys.

Barbara Cains *Age 13*

Craig Gibbons *Age 6*

Oldies should do more sit-ups

My advice to everyone who wants to keep healthy. Jog for about one mile. If you can't jog, do some sit ups. About 400 every day.

Danny Leamon *Age 8*

When my nana tries to touch her tooes she fell over and hurt her back.

Mandy Winters *Age 10*

People shoad doow exercises so they keep looking young.
If you don't you will get fat and your heart mit slow down and you will be ill and you mit dide.

Andrew Tomlinson *Age 8*

Grandad goes for long walks to keep his legs in shape.

Mark Saunders *Age 11*

Andrew Purser Age 6

Never mind, poor old thing

Did you go to the dentists on Wednesday, how many teeth did he take out? Oh that's alright if he only took out one. It was your last tooth? Oh well you can't win them all.

Michael Eastman *Age 11*

If a person's teeth are falling out you could say, well at least you will be rich. You will get some money from the tooth fairy. Also you could exercise just by blowing out all the candles on your birthday cake every birthday.

Michael Amey *Age 10*

Growing old is what everyone is doing, though you may not think so. You are not going to age much when you are fifty or sixty but just realize that, in fact, you have been growing so old that it shows.

Katie Edgington *Age 14*

Oh! Antie Milly never mind about your wrinkly neck and your wrinkled face. I will still cuddle you and kiss you. You have lots of company because you are kind and the children who visit you don't mind one bite your shackey hands and a bite of your mastosh.

Donna Greenaway

Resolutions for when I'm old

I won't pat my grandchildren on the head every time I see them and say, "My, how you've grown."

Dolores Marino *Age 14*

When I'm very old, I won't make my grandchildren do as they're told, I'll spoil them rotten.

Tabitha Gardiner *Age 14*

When I'm a grandma I won't start every sentence with, "When I was a girl".

Sarah Gardner *Age 14*

When I'm 92, I'll bore everyone by telling them how things cost nothing when I was little. I'll tell them about life before computers.

Helena Rodriguez

When I'm older, I shall not grouse about the price of everything for hours on end.

Meryl Dellocano *Age 14*

Dominic Ashton Age 7

Nina Wright

My great, great aunt is eighty-two. She sews a lot and hopes to live for a very, very long time so that she can finish all her sewing!

Zoë Upton *Age 9*

Why do grandmas have to get older? Why can't they stay with their soft wrinkled skin? Why can't they stay with their old white hair?

Sara Ford *Age 11*

We like the old ones

Really old people are terrific.
They tell stories of their lives and are
always saying "When I was
young..."

Sarah Davison Age 13

I Lovit
wen-
they tell
me wote
theydid
wenthey
wer
Little.

Stuart Whittington Age 7

The advantages...

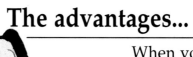

When you are older
you can swim better
because booze makes you fat
and you will float better.
Samuel Ross *Age 8*

At least when I'm old
I won't have to
put away all my toys
every night.
Billy Patulski *Age 10*

Iain Jones *Age 7*

You do not have to use
your brains so much
because they are a bit
rusty.
Karen Edwards _Age 10_

In a way it must be great
to get old because you get
an opportunity to stay in
bed all day.
Genevieve Wright _Age 10_

Everyone respects you and
no one would have the heart
to tell you to shut up when
you started rambling on about
what the old days were like
for the umpteenth time.
Susan Williams _Age 14_

The joys of old age

The happiest things about growing old are seeing again the beauty of spring, the browns, greens and falling leaves of autumn, and the feel of crisp snow in winter. It is also the joy of seeing grandchildren, great grandchildren and new young life, and teaching them and showing them the mysteries and wonders that each day brings.

Gillian Threadingham Age 14

When it is my Grandma's birthday she does not want it for the presents and the big dinner, but for the pleasure of seeing the family again.

Mark Anderson

People need people, but the longing is more in old age.

Jennifer Cowasji Age 13

Grandparents like other peoples birthdays in a different way. They like people's birthdays if they know they're happy. They're happy to see the other person happy.

David Larkin Age 9

Charlotte Parnaby *Age 7*

Young at heart

Some people think when they have those dreaded wrinkles they are old. That's crazy! It depends totally on you. You may not look the same but if you want you can act twenty years younger.

Cassandra Garner Age 14

Old people are good at exagarating. But deep down they are young. There harts still containe love.

Stuart Berry Age 9

Wouldn't it be great if every one could live for ever especially Grandmas and Granddads because they bring lots of pleasure.

Angus Newhouse Age 11

eat your heart out Damon Hill

Go Grandma

Nicholas Age 9

Sharon Murphy *Age 6*

I'll do roly-polys in the snow when I'm 87

Is it fun at 87?

James Davis Age 12

I think I'll go wild when
I'm old and be quite eccentric.
Yes, I'd like that!
I'll go singing in the rain,
(something I've always wanted to do)
with bright yellow galoshes on and a red hat.
People don't mind what you do
When you're old, they just say,
"Poor old dear, she's not got long to go,"
And tap their heads.
So you see I could do all the things
I've always wanted to do,
but couldn't do,
because I was young.
Be like a little child at eighty-seven.
Jump in haystacks
And pick flowers from other people's gardens.
Do roly-polys in the snow.
I could have quite a bit of fun,
when I'm old.

Lisa Burnage Age 14

Granma died when she was weard out

Mary

Mark Keene Age 10

When they die
they will be buffed
in a Cafein and
When god comes
you will be ll Alive
and you
cam made a
cup of tea

Steven Blake

Aggh

50   60